Art Matters
11-14

Jeff Orgee

Heinemann

Heinemann Educational Publishers
Halley Court, Jordan Hill, Oxford OX2 8EJ
a division of Reed Educational and Professional Publishing Ltd.
Heinemann is a registered trademark of Reed Educational and Professional Publishing Ltd.

OXFORD   MELBOURNE   AUCKLAND
KAMPALA   JOHANNESBURG   BLANTYRE   GABORONE
IBADAN   PORTSMOUTH (NH) USA   CHICAGO

First published 1999

03 02 01
10 9 8 7 6 5 4 3 2

British Library Cataloguing in Publication Data
A catalogue record for this book is available from the British Library

ISBN 0 435 81204 1

Designed and typeset by Artistix, Thame, Oxon
Printed and bound in Spain by Edelvives

Acknowledgements
The author would like to thank the pupils of Kinloss School, Martley, Worcestershire, for their kind assistance in providing artwork in the making of this publication.

The publishers would like to thank the following for permission to use photographs:
Gary Green, p. 5 (bottom right), courtesy of the artist; p. 8 (top): Paul Klee Stiftung, Bern, copyright © DACS 2000; p. 8 (bottom): private collection, copyright © DACS 2000; p. 9 (top): AKG London; private collection, p. 9 (bottom); p. 10 (both): courtesy of the artist; p. 16 (top): courtesy of the artist; p. 28 (top left): Suzanne DeMott Gaadt; p. 28 (bottom left) courtesy of the Trustees of the V & A/photographer Daniel McGrath; p. 28 (bottom right) courtesy of the Trustees of the V & A; p. 36 (top): © 1999 Cordon Art B.V. – Baarn – Holland – all rights reserved; p. 40 (top left) copyright The National Trust/Photographer Mike Williams; p. 40 (bottom left): Topkapi Palace, Istanbul © Sonia Halliday Photographs; p. 40 (bottom right): photographer: Bobby Hanson; p. 40 (top right): private collection; p. 44 (top): Collection of The University of Arizona Museum of Art, Tucson. Gift of Oliver James, © ARS, NY and DACS, London 2000; p. 44 (bottom): AKG London, © Mondrian/Holztman Trust, c/o Beeldrecht, Amsterdam, Holland/DACS 2000; p. 48: The Museum of Modern Art, New York. Purchase. Photograph © 1999 The Museum of Modern Art, New York, © DACS, London, 2000; p. 55 (top): © The British Museumn, London; p. 60: AKG London.

The publishers have made every effort to trace copyright holders. However, if any material has been incorrectly acknowledged, we would be pleased to correct this at the earliest opportunity.

Contents

Year 7

1 Tone and form 4
2 Line and linear drawing 8
3 Colour 12
4 Ceramic fish 16
5 Ears and eyes 20
6 Paper sculpture 24

Year 8

1 Knots and ropes 28
2 Flight 32
3 Reflections 36
4 Tile sets 40
5 Fruit cross-sections 44
6 Viewpoints 48

Year 9

1 Masks 52
2 Insects 56
3 Tone and landscape 60

Glossary 64

Tone and form

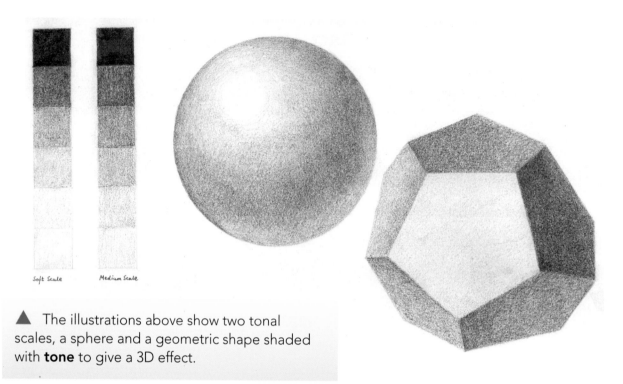

Soft Scale   Medium Scale

▲ The illustrations above show two tonal scales, a sphere and a geometric shape shaded with **tone** to give a 3D effect.

◀ This is a **conté** drawing by Georges Seurat, drawn in about 1883. It is a preliminary drawing for the painting called 'Une Baignade' which is in the National Gallery in London. The artist has captured the subtle **graduation** of tones by using conté on textured paper.

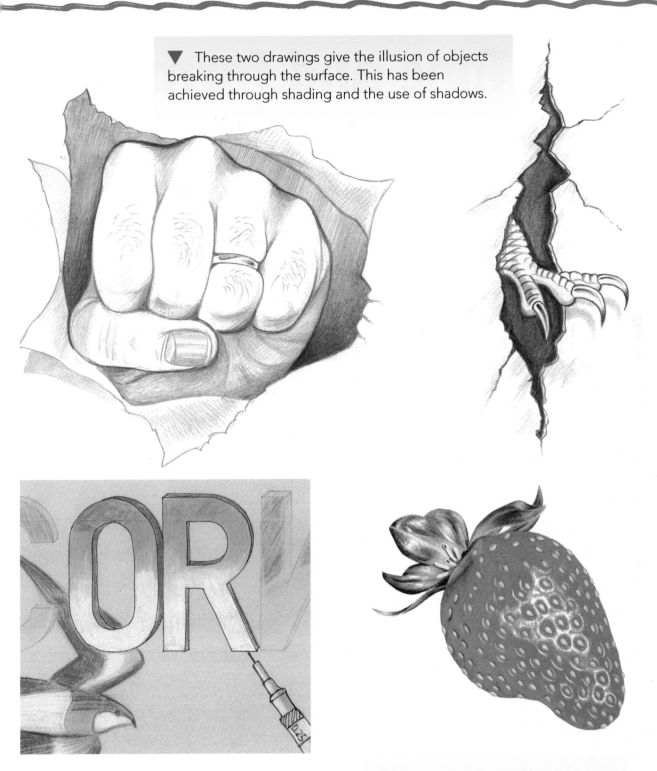

▼ These two drawings give the illusion of objects breaking through the surface. This has been achieved through shading and the use of shadows.

▲ This section of a pupil's folder has lettering produced with a graduated tone. A pen is shown in the process of filling in.

▲ This strawberry was drawn by the artist Gary Greene in 1996 using coloured pencils. It is an excellent example of **blending** and **burnishing** to create strong colour.

Tone and form

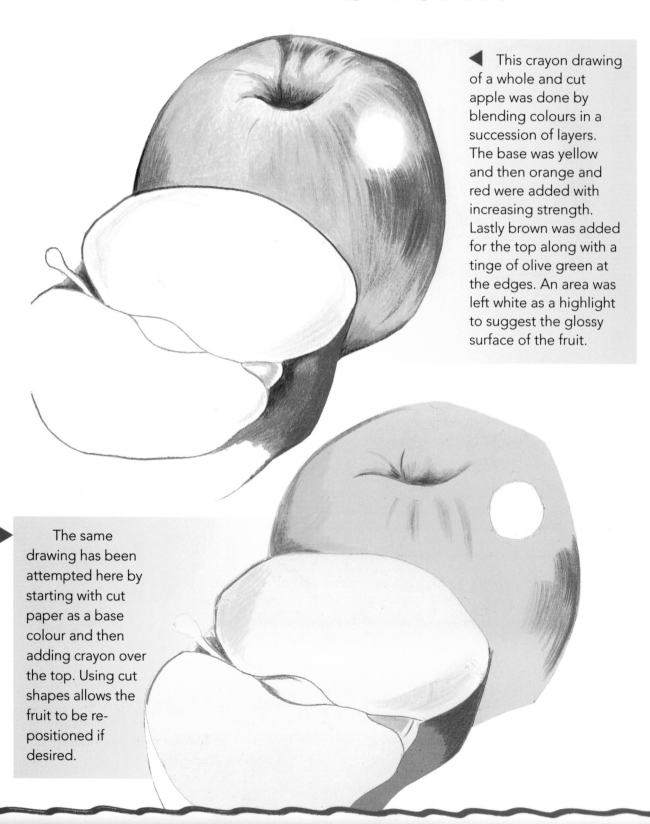

This crayon drawing of a whole and cut apple was done by blending colours in a succession of layers. The base was yellow and then orange and red were added with increasing strength. Lastly brown was added for the top along with a tinge of olive green at the edges. An area was left white as a highlight to suggest the glossy surface of the fruit.

The same drawing has been attempted here by starting with cut paper as a base colour and then adding crayon over the top. Using cut shapes allows the fruit to be re-positioned if desired.

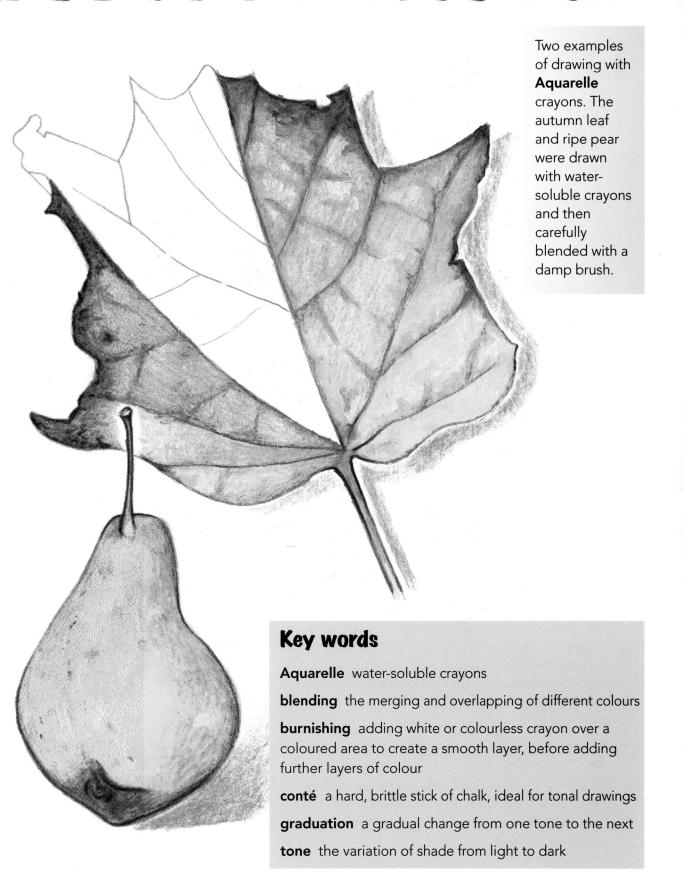

Two examples of drawing with **Aquarelle** crayons. The autumn leaf and ripe pear were drawn with water-soluble crayons and then carefully blended with a damp brush.

Key words

Aquarelle water-soluble crayons

blending the merging and overlapping of different colours

burnishing adding white or colourless crayon over a coloured area to create a smooth layer, before adding further layers of colour

conté a hard, brittle stick of chalk, ideal for tonal drawings

graduation a gradual change from one tone to the next

tone the variation of shade from light to dark

Line and linear drawing

Paul Klee (1879-1940) produced thousands of line drawings during his artistic career. Many are experimental and appear to be playful doodles. It was as the artist himself expressed it: 'Like taking a line for a walk'.

▲ The above example is called 'Game on the water'. It was drawn in pen during 1935. A face appears mysteriously out of the waves of the sea, by using **continuous** (unbroken) **lines** to suggest the movement of the water.

▶ The second example shows the figure of a jester. Klee has done this simple line drawing probably without taking his pen off the paper. There is little detail yet the continuous line reflects the movement and excitement of the figure.

These two pen drawings are by Vincent van Gogh (1853–1890).
They were drawn using a pencil, quill and a reed pen, with Indian ink.

▲ This landscape of Arles, in France, was drawn in the summer of 1888. The drawing shows a whole variety of marks from fine to bold, with **stippling**, continuous and broken lines.

▶ The portrait of Patience Escalier was drawn in 1888 and again demonstrates a whole range of marks. There is a strong contrast between the background texture achieved with the reed pen and the **cross-hatching** and fine lines used on the face, drawn with a quill.

Line and linear drawing

This page shows two examples of wildlife illustrations done by the artist and naturalist Norman Hickin in the 1970s.

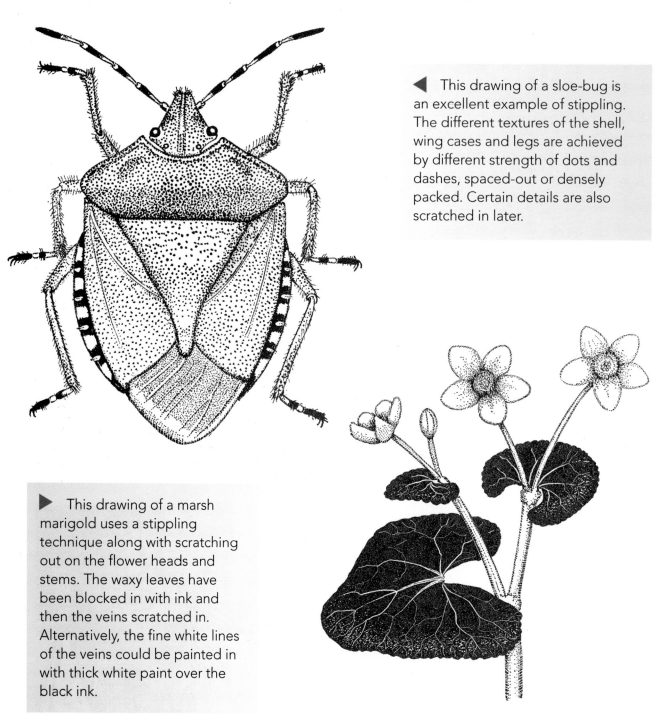

◀ This drawing of a sloe-bug is an excellent example of stippling. The different textures of the shell, wing cases and legs are achieved by different strength of dots and dashes, spaced-out or densely packed. Certain details are also scratched in later.

▶ This drawing of a marsh marigold uses a stippling technique along with scratching out on the flower heads and stems. The waxy leaves have been blocked in with ink and then the veins scratched in. Alternatively, the fine white lines of the veins could be painted in with thick white paint over the black ink.

'Line Drawing.'

~ Andrew Oates ~

These line drawings of fungi were drawn by pupils with a fine marker pen, using a wide range of **textural** marks, along with a decorative border.

Richard Annison

Key words

continuous line a drawing done without taking the point off the page

cross-hatching lines set at an angle to build up a denser texture or tone

stippling a drawing made up of points and dots

textural describing surface effects

Colour

▶ The top painting shows a completed colour wheel, in watercolour, with the **primary** and **secondary colours** on the inner circle, and the **tertiary colours** on the outer circle. To do this you need to be accurate and mix the colours cleanly.

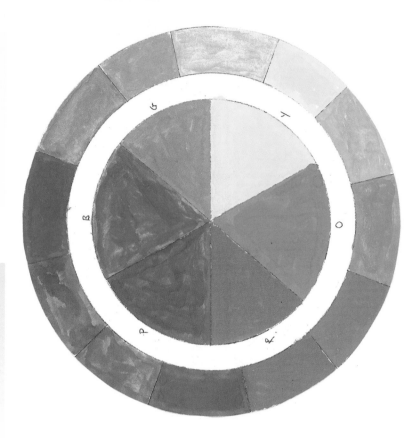

▼ The three **tint** and **shade** scales below have been done by gradually shading the three primary colours by adding black and then gradually tinting by adding white. Subtle variation of colour can be achieved by careful mixing.

▲ Two examples of a landscape painted using only **transparent washes** of black watercolour. The top study has been painted using a visual aid key line as a guide. The bottom piece has been painted using only a very feint pencil sketch.

Colour

◀ This watercolour study of a rose has been painted with different shades of one colour, alizarin crimson, in various strengths with more or less water. It has been painted 'wet into wet', where the washes are allowed to run into each other.

▲ Two versions of Edvard Munch's 'The Scream' have been painted by filling in a keyline drawing with tints and shades of just the primary colours, to add to the tension of the picture. The pupils have tried to mix subtle differences in colour.

▶ This is a **limited palette** copy of a portrait by the Italian artist Antonello da Messina, painted in **opaque** colours. Two colours were used: yellow ochre and burnt sienna along with black and white. With careful mixing a whole range of colours was achieved.

Key words

limited palette   a restricted range of colours which are intermixed

opaque   more pigment is used, so that you can't see through the colour

primary colours   the key non-mixed colours: red, yellow and blue

secondary colours   colours mixed by combining two primary colours: orange, purple and green

shades   colours mixed by adding black

tertiary colours   colours mixed by combining adjacent secondary and primary colours

tints   colours mixed by adding white

transparent   see-through (e.g. washes that are thinly applied)

wash   a very watery mix applied with a large brush

Ceramic fish

▲ This illustration is an excellent example of a trout by the artist and illustrator Rod Sutterby. The artist has used a combination of materials (including crayon, pastel, paint and pencil) to capture the silvery texture of the scales and the glossy eye.

▶ This illustration of a skate has been drawn primarily in crayon. The pupil who drew this has taken care to capture the pattern on the tail and body. Some tonal shading has been added to show the 3D form of the creature, while the pupil has indicated two cut-away sections to act as containers.

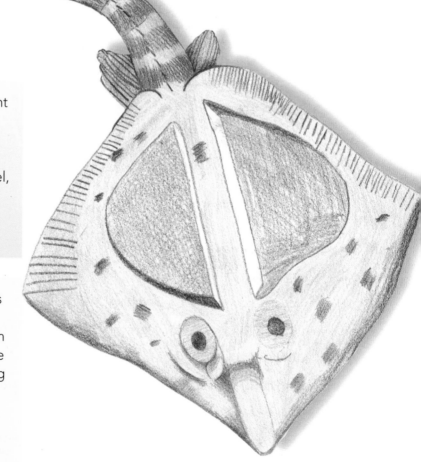

▶ This drawing of an angel-fish was done using **mixed media**, with a combination of crayon, watercolour and pencil. Thicker white watercolour was used over the base crayon work, to add the scales, lips and reflections in the eye.

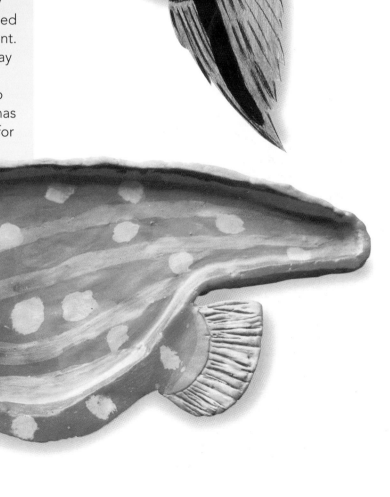

▼ This finished ceramic fish shows **modelled** and **incised** details. A round shape was pressed into the soft clay for the eye, while the fins show incised details scratched in with a sharp point. One compartment has been cut away at a lower level to hold objects or sweets. Ready-mixed colours add to the exotic nature of the fish, and it has been finished off with clear varnish for a glossy effect.

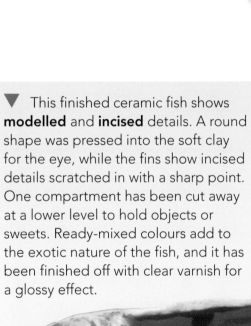

Ceramic fish

◀ This ceramic fish has several compartments. The shape of the sections adds to the pattern of the fish. Each section has been decorated with a different combination of pattern and colour.

◀ This photo shows a good example of how pressed and incised decoration can successfully provide the scales and lines of the fins. The container has been provided by adding a small thrown shape, which has been decorated on its rim. The colour has been added with an airbrush, using acrylic inks.

◀ This sea horse is a ceramic sculpture modelled in clay. Details have been built up, along with incised markings around the eye. The whole creature has been painted with a base coat of blue acrylic with selected details edged in gold.

Key words

incised cut away, scratched or inscribed, with a sharp point or by pressing

mixed media a combination of different materials, e.g. crayon with watercolour

modelling using clay to build up shape and form

Ears and eyes

▶ This clay profile shows a small section of the face including the ear, side-burns and hair. The ear has been built up off the surface with parts cut away to create a 3D effect. Different textural effects have been added for the different hair lengths – for example, the close-cropped hair of the beard and the waves of hair behind the ear. This has been achieved using the point of a clay-modelling tool.

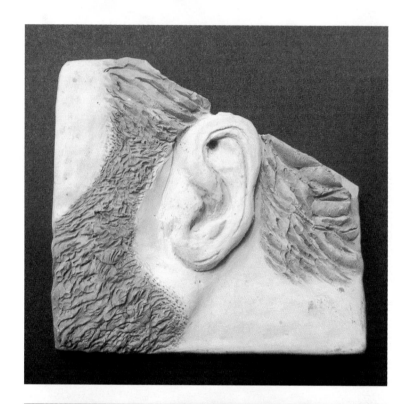

▶ This clay profile contains some interesting details such as a peaked hat, sunglasses, earrings and a moustache. An attempt has been made also to build up the contours of the face by adding thin layers of extra clay on to the base shape.

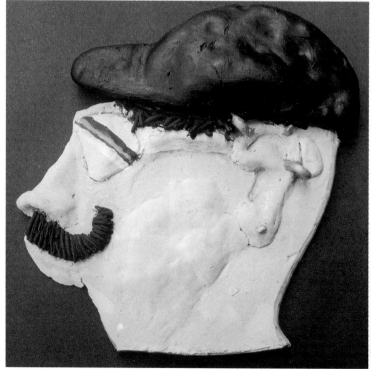

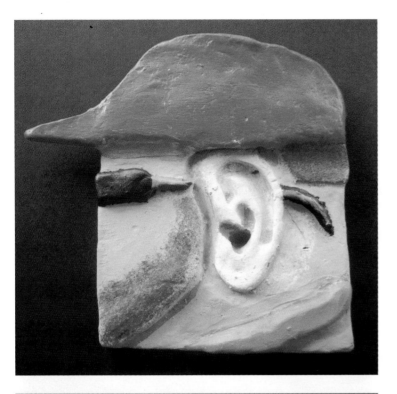

◀ This clay profile shows an attempt to give a 3D look to a shallow surface, by building up the cheek, hat, collar and hair from the base shape. Colour has been added with a stippling brush for the texture of the beard and hair.

◀ This clay profile is a good example of different textural treatments for the hair and beard. The hair has been modelled, whereas the beard has been stippled. A hat with a rim has been modelled and finished with clear varnish.

Ears and eyes

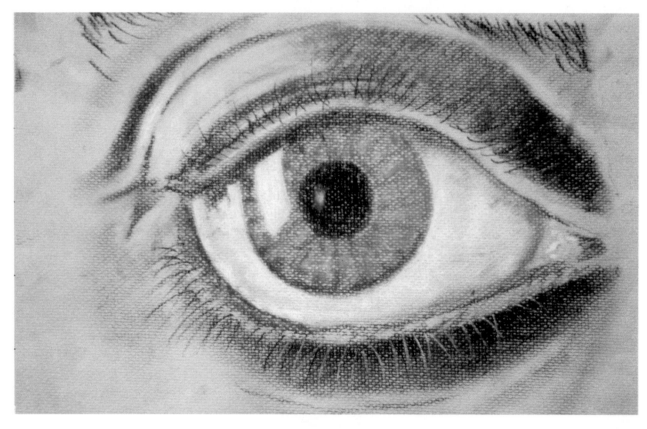

These two pastel eyes are based on a print by M. C. Escher produced in 1946. They have been drawn using chalk pastels on a coloured, textured paper. The colour has been applied using the broad side and the end of the stick. Paper towelling has been used to create a smooth blend wherever needed.

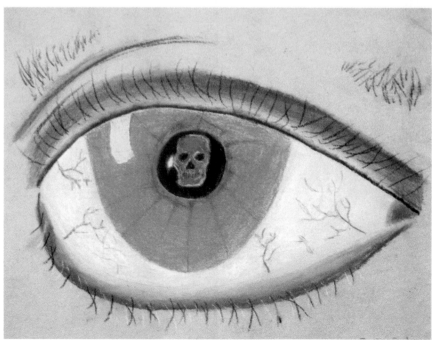

This large **frottage** uses the eye as a mysterious floating object in an imaginary landscape. The composition includes a whole range of textures derived from everyday objects such as concrete slabs, wooden planks and the pattern on frosted glass. The possibilities are endless.

Key word

frottage an image made by combining rubbings from various textures

Paper sculpture

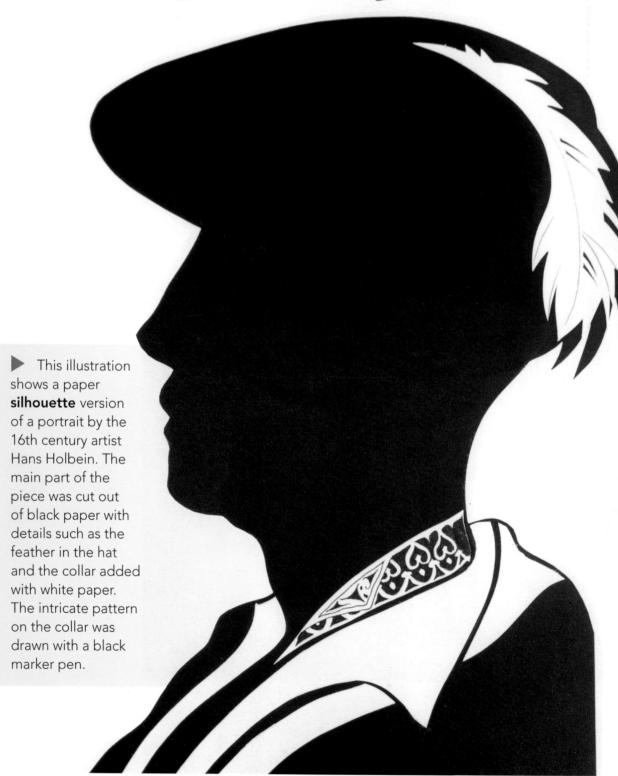

▶ This illustration shows a paper **silhouette** version of a portrait by the 16th century artist Hans Holbein. The main part of the piece was cut out of black paper with details such as the feather in the hat and the collar added with white paper. The intricate pattern on the collar was drawn with a black marker pen.

Here, the same portrait of Simon George of Cornwall by Hans Holbein has been developed from the silhouette into a paper sculpture. Thin layers are built up to give a 3D effect. Cut lines are used to give texture to the hair. Sections such as the neck, moustache and ear are scored and folded. The play of light and shadow adds to the 3D effect.

This section of a scarlet macaw is an example of what can be achieved with paper sculpture. Paper and card have been pre-coloured before cutting into feather shapes. The feathers are then assembled into a wing by gluing them to a base that remains out of sight. The face and beak are thin layers of overlapped coloured paper.

Paper sculpture

◀ This illustration is an interpretation of a sculptured head by Pablo Picasso. It is constructed out of reinforced cardboard from one sheet and is able to stand unsupported. Facial features have been added with extra card and string. The finished head has been painted with poster colours.

▶ This second head is also based on a Picasso sheet-metal piece, and has also been made from one piece of reinforced card. It can also be viewed **'in-the-round'**. Here facial features have been achieved by painting rather than by adding extra materials.

Key words

in-the-round   a 3D sculpture that can be viewed from several angles, not just in relief

low-relief   a shallow sculpture made up of successive layers

silhouette   a shape or figure blacked-out against a strong light

▶   This paper sculpture, done by a pupil, is a fine example of how a 3D effect can be created with successive layers of overlapping card and paper. The various sections have been pre-coloured with an airbrush and paint before assembly. Invisible supports have been put in place to raise the various parts of the body off the background. The result is a **low-relief** sculpture that appears deeper than it actually is.

27

Knots and ropes

▲ An example of a Celtic 'everlasting knot' design.

▲ An example of an Islamic interlocking design.

▲ A 19th century **pattern-repeat** design by William Morris.

▲ A 19th century pattern-repeat design by Charles Voysey.

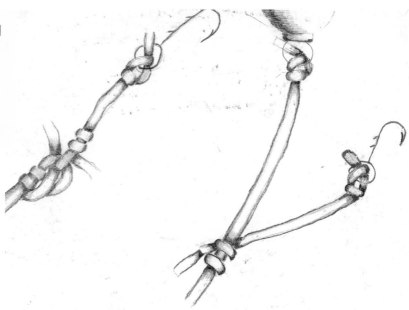

▶ This pupil has experimented with a number of knots and combinations, linking the knots with hooks. These were drawn out on to an A3 sheet and modelled with tone.

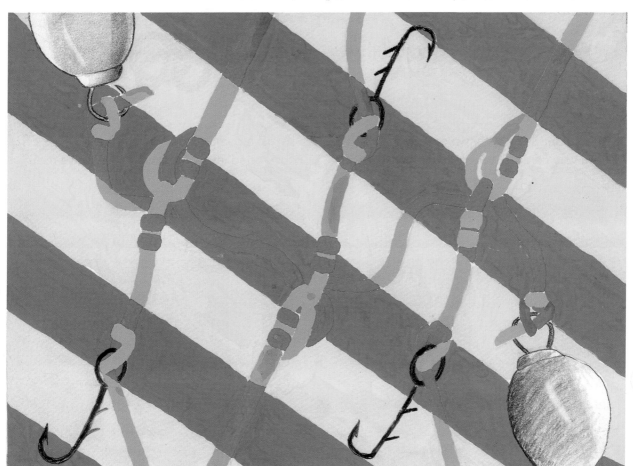

▲ The sketches were then developed into a finished design, set against a contrasting background pattern, and incorporating hooks and weights as used in fishing.

Knots and ropes

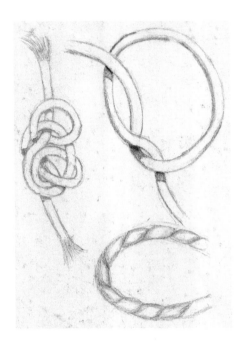

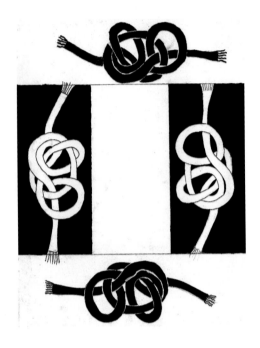

▲ An idea sheet with two copies of knots and a very complex original design for a knot.

▲ The complex design was then developed into a negative and positive motif.

▶ Two finished designs using the idea of alternating **complementary colours**, painted in a hard-edged, **flat colour** on to a six-square grid.

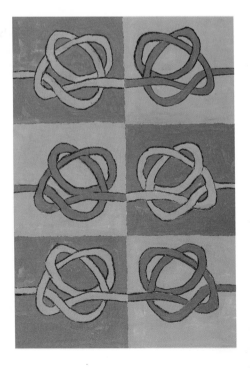

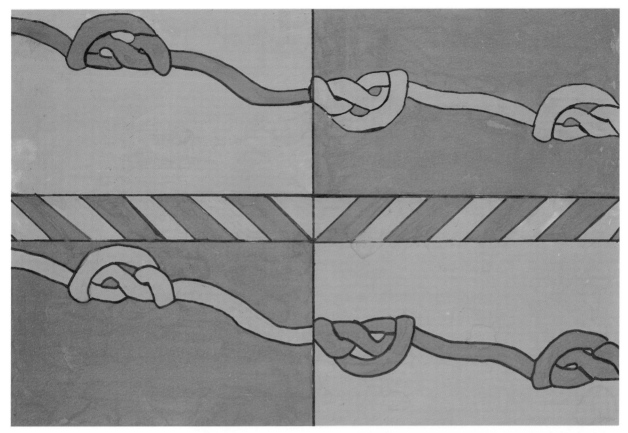

▲ A finished design where the repeating idea links from one 'tile' to the next.

▶ In this example the pupil has converted a linking design into a simple block-print, using thick card on a base, inked up and printed over a colour-faded background.

Key words

complementary colours colours that are opposite each other on the colour wheel: red and green, purple and yellow, blue and orange

flat colour colour painted in a smooth opaque technique

pattern-repeat where a design has been repeated over an area, often linking together in a continuous pattern

Flight

◀ This fruit bat has been made out of one section of card, with care taken to capture the contrasting texture of the body and the thin, paper-like wings. A mixture of crayon, felt-tip and watercolour has been used. Sections of the wings have been scored and folded to give a 3D effect. The feet are made out of wire and the bat hangs from a bamboo pole by its feet.

▲ This card sculpture of a flying puffin has been constructed out of four flat sections. The colour was added to the sections before assembly. Black ready-mixed paint was used to block in the wings and body. Watercolour was used for the detail of the face. The silvery sand eels were sprayed with an airbrush. The sections were glued together with a glue gun and suspended with fishing line.

▶ This black-headed gull is a card sculpture made from four sections. The painting of the bird has concentrated on the upper wings, capturing the changing shades of grey and black. Berol semi-moist paint tubs were used, mixed to an opaque consistency, which dried to a flat colour on the white card. The bird was suspended at an angle to allow the upper wings to be seen clearly, as in a gliding position.

▲ This wooden toucan was made out of four sections of 4 mm plywood cut with a jigsaw. The cut shapes were painted with acrylics because watercolours would sink into the wood and leave a dull finish. The wings were attached to the body with strong fishing line at a point that made the bird balanced. The wings were then attached by line to a thin wooden pole, which kept the wings apart. If pulled from beneath, the bird flies under its own steam for quite a while.

Flight

◀ This beautiful **ceramic plaque** is a fine example of how to suggest space and depth with thin successive layers, built up in relief. The bat is the top layer and the night sky is the base layer, with the church, moon and trees making up the intermediate layers. The fired plaque has been painted in acrylics and the moon coated in a layer of clear varnish.

▼ As an alternative to the 'flight' theme this pupil has constructed a mini pick-up truck on a ramp, as though in take-off position. It has a full load of logs. It has been fired and painted in acrylics.

▶ This detailed ceramic plaque is a good example of how to suggest distance with only three layers. The fulmar is shown gliding effortlessly over steep cliffs, with a choppy sea below. The different textures suggested by modelling are evident: the smoothness of the bird, the receding choppy surface of the water, the craggy surface of the cliff-face and the pitted quality of the cliff-top. Considerable time has been taken in observing and painting the plumage of the sea bird.

Key word

ceramic plaque
a shallow-relief ceramic sculpture of different levels

Reflections

▲ This example of M. C. Escher's work shows the effects of reflective glass. He not only records the reflected image but also shows the **image distortion** created by a three-dimensional surface.

▶ A metal cylinder captures an image of the world around it, in this case a desert scene. One example has been rendered in crayon. The other has been produced using an airbrush with touches of white **gouache**.

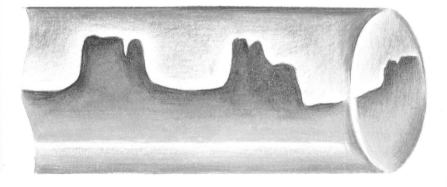

This page shows two examples of capturing reflective effects in glass objects by using different materials.

◀ The wineglass has been drawn with biro, which is ideal for recording the distortions and fluid nature of the reflections.

▶ This perfume bottle has been drawn with crayons on to black paper. With this method the pupil is actually drawing with light and capturing how the light hits the surfaces of the bottle. For intense areas of light, small amounts of white gouache have been added.

Reflections

▶ A ceramic teapot has been drawn in four different materials: biro, **graphite stick**, conté and watercolour. Each material records the reflections and distortions in its own way.

BIRO · CONTÉ · GRAPHITE STICK · WATERCOLOUR

▲ A detailed still-life drawing in crayon on to a textured paper, with a number of contrasting textures. The bottle and glass distort the objects behind them.

▲ A **collage** version of the same still life, reduced to just black and white.

Here are two examples of reflections in water, created using an airbrush and paper **templates** or **masks**. Details such as rigging have been added after with an Edding pen.

Key words

collage an image made up of cut paper pieces pasted on for a tonal or colour effect

gouache thick, opaque watercolour, which dries flat

graphite stick a compact strip of graphite with no wood, ideal for dark, tonal shading

image distortion the way an image is broken up when viewed through glass or water

template or **mask** a shape cut out of paper, used to duplicate a design or shape as either a negative or a positive image

Tile sets

This page shows four examples of *figurative* and non-figurative tile designs from various times and cultures.

▲ Medieval tiles from the 14th century with **heraldic** motifs.

▲ A Victorian tile from the 19th century, based on medieval designs.

▲ An Islamic tile design of interlocking motifs, from southern Spain.

▲ A modern figurative tile from the USA.

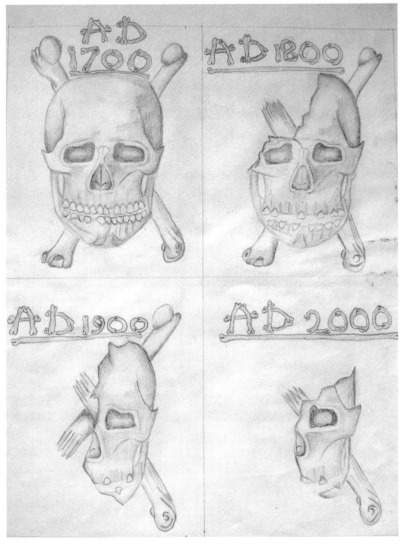

◀ This design shows the idea of an image changing gradually from one tile to the next, to suggest the passing of time. The finished tile was modelled by cutting away from an initially thicker tile of 15 mm thickness.

▼ This is the original design for a set of two elephant tiles. The design has been done as an outline. A section has been chosen to show a suggested colour scheme.

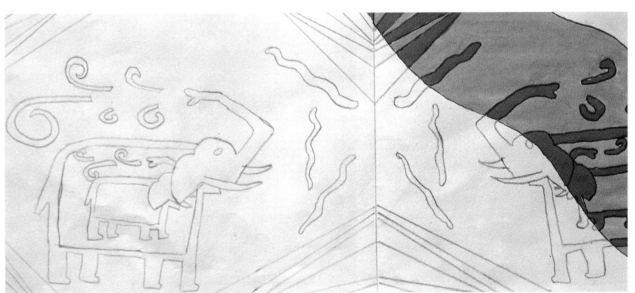

Tile sets

▶ Here the pupil has made a set of four tiles that link together in a **geometric design**. The central section is unglazed, revealing an incised design. Other geometric features are built up in a low relief. The design shows the influence of medieval tile-makers.

▼ This illustration shows two tiles from a set of four that the pupil made from a symmetrical design. The cobras face each other in a linking design. The snake on the left is built up in relief with areas cut away. The snake on the right has been incised with features raised. The base is undecorated and the snakes have been finished in acrylics.

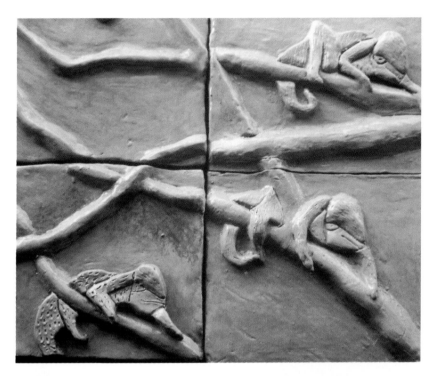

◀ This is a set of four tiles where the branches link from one tile to the next. The lizards have been modelled separately and added to the branches. The set has been finished with a gloss pewter glaze.

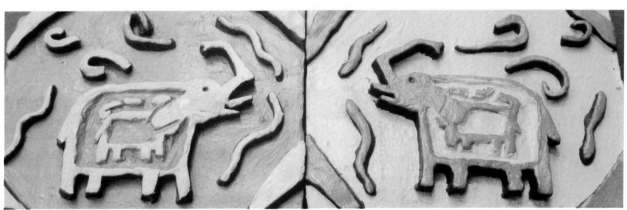

▲ The elephants and background designs are all in relief. They have been modelled separately and then added to the base tile. They have been finished with watercolour in an opposite contrast and then coated with a matt varnish.

Key words

figurative design a design consisting of recognizable forms

geometric design a design composed of abstract shapes

heraldic design a design incorporating details associated with a coat of arms/medieval motifs

Fruit cross-sections

◀ This is an oil painting by the American artist Georgia O'Keeffe. It illustrates a close-up view of the Red Canna flower, practically as a bee would view it, looking through the inner workings, twisting and turning through the folding petals. The shapes and patterns of the flower have been simplified into a dramatic composition that emphasizes the exciting combination of line, tone and colour.

'Red Canna' by Georgia O'Keeffe, oil on canvas, 1923

▶ In this painting by the Dutch artist Piet Mondrian we can easily recognize the shape of a tree, but it is interesting to see how the artist has stressed the horizontal patterns and shapes of the branches. In exaggerating these patterns the artist left out precise detail for the overall effect.

'Horizontal Tree' by Piet Mondrian, 1911

A pyramid shaped *viewfinder* was placed over the original tomato drawing shown on this page to select the most interesting area.

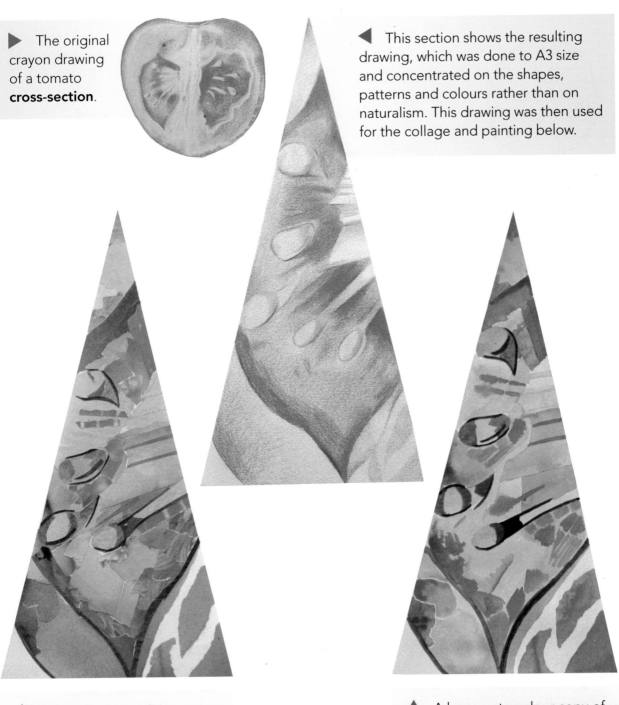

▶ The original crayon drawing of a tomato **cross-section**.

◀ This section shows the resulting drawing, which was done to A3 size and concentrated on the shapes, patterns and colours rather than on naturalism. This drawing was then used for the collage and painting below.

▲ A large collage of the enlarged section. Care has been taken to ensure accuracy of colour.

▲ A large watercolour copy of the collage, using wet-into-wet techniques to encourage the colours to bleed.

Fruit cross-sections

▲ The original crayon drawing of an orange cross-section.

◀ In this crayon drawing the pupil has selected a small section of the orange to investigate and has emphasized the fibrous texture of the fruit, while exaggerating the radiating pattern like spokes in a wheel.

▲ An alternative idea is to produce a simple stencil-print, where the colour and pattern has been reduced to an absolute minimum.

▲ The original drawing of a lemon cross-section.

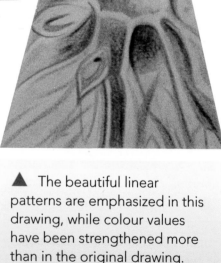

▲ The beautiful linear patterns are emphasized in this drawing, while colour values have been strengthened more than in the original drawing.

In the previous two pages a pyramid viewfinder was used to select areas for enlargement. This page shows how other shapes can be used.

▲ This juice carton shows how illustrations made using a viewfinder can be developed into a **graphical** application. The design can be scanned or redrawn to size and combined with type and graphics for a professional looking result.

Key words

cross-section   an object cut through to show its internal structure

graphical   the combination of type, illustration and layout in a design

viewfinder   a piece of card with a hole cut in it for selecting an area of an image for closer scrutiny

Viewpoints

'Nostalgia of the Infinite' by Giorgio de Chirico, oil on canvas, 1913

◄ This painting is by the artist Giorgio de Chirico, who is recognized as one of the forerunners of the **Surrealist movement**. It is a dramatic painting, which uses a low viewpoint, to stress the dominating tower. The two figures give us an idea of scale, yet the people are faceless. There are long creeping shadows due to a strong sidelight which highlights the tower in sharp focus. A shadow crosses the square from an unseen object or building. The whole atmosphere of the painting is one of threat and unease.

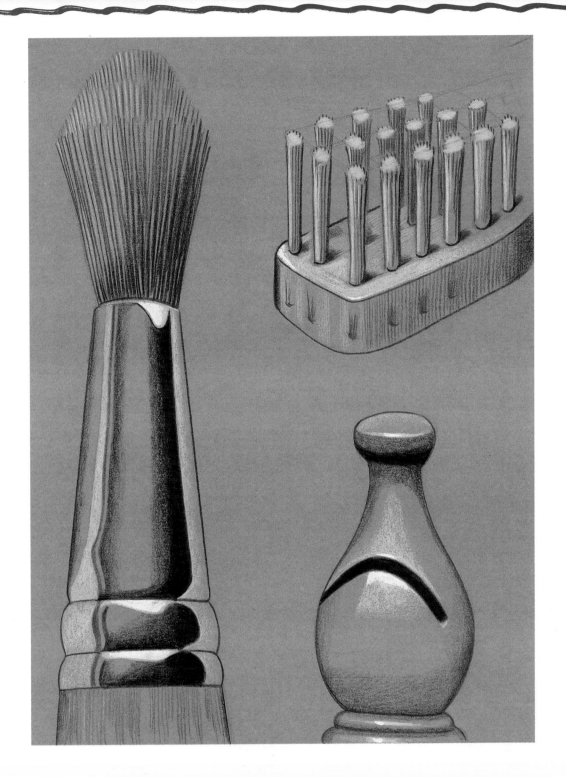

▲ Three everyday and familiar objects have been drawn here: a large watercolour paintbrush, a bishop chess-piece and the head of a toothbrush. Only a portion of each object has been drawn and effort has been taken to capture the texture, pattern and light of the object. The drawing has been done on grey paper with black and white crayon, with a touch of white gouache for intense areas of light.

Viewpoints

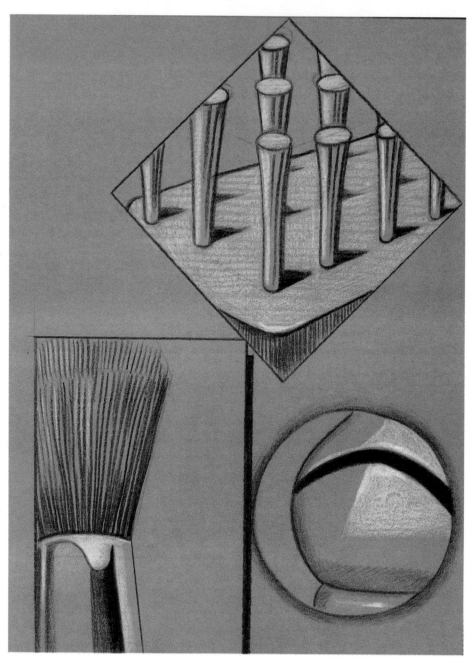

▲ Here the same three objects have been drawn with the use of a viewfinder to select even smaller sections to draw in detail. Three different-shaped viewfinders have been used. It now becomes increasingly difficult to recognize the true identity of the objects. The drawing has been done using black and white crayon on to grey paper, but charcoal or pastel work well on a larger scale.

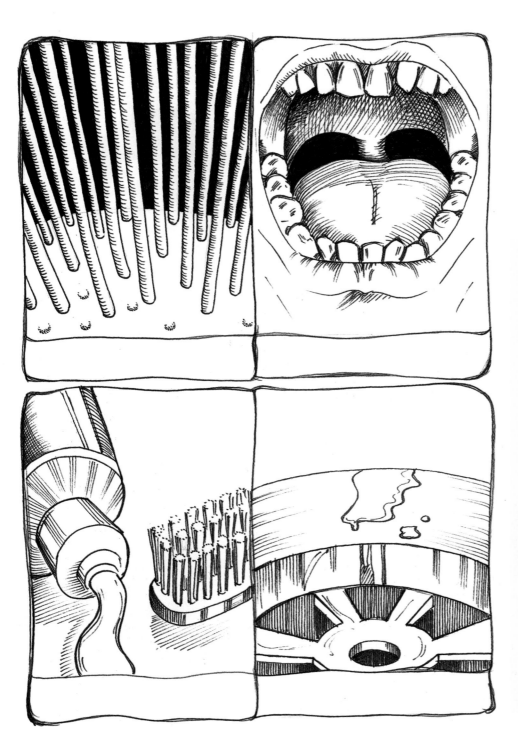

These illustrations are part of a cartoon strip that traces the journey of someone who has been shrunk to a very small size. Everyday objects and situations take on a different viewpoint and scale. A head of hair is now a forest, a mouth becomes a dark cave and a plug-hole is transformed into a bottomless pit.

Key word

Surrealist movement a group of artists whose work featured real objects placed out of their usual role or in unusual combinations

Masks

▲ A finished self-portrait drawn to A3 size, modelled with tone for a 3D effect.

▲ A **brush-drawn** over-painting, with a copy of the original portrait as a base.

▲ A brush-drawn over-painting that totally changes the age of the sitter.

▲ A **lino-print** based on the over-painting, printed on to a **distressed** background.

◀ A lino-print on to black paper then hand-coloured with soft crayon.

▶ A lino-print on to black paper then hand-coloured to accentuate the markings.

▶ A 3D ceramic mask made from a thin slab of moulded clay with marbles for eyes.

▲ A 3D ceramic mask made from slabbed clay, finished with gold acrylic.

Key words

brush-drawing painting in a linear style with the tip of the brush

distressing ageing a support by sponging and stippling, etc.

lino-print a print taken off the raised, inked-up surface of a linoleum tile

Masks

Mask cultures

Japan has a tremendous tradition of mask-making for its many dramas and theatres. Most striking are the masks for the characters in the classic Noh theatre. Simple and bold in style, they are carved from one piece of wood, and coloured to accentuate the 3D quality, with eyes and mouth cut out and outlined in ink.

▲ A modern copy of a 17th century Japanese Noh mask, made in cardboard, painted and varnished.

The mask sits on the front of the face, the actor bringing the character alive by his convincing performance. The characters include a demon, a god or deity, a lunatic, men and women.

▶ A modern Japanese mask, made from papier mâché, painted and varnished.

Africa has one of the richest mask cultures in the world, with strong tribal and regional styles. The mask below has been made by an Akamba craftsman. It has accentuated ears and skin markings, meant to represent a Masai tribesman. Many masks are now made in East Africa for the tourist trade.

▲ A Mexican stone mask, c. 300–650 BCE.

This Mexican mask is the oldest example shown here, and dates from between 300–650 BCE. It is thought to have been used for funerals. Masks of this type are sometimes found decorated with mother of pearl and coral mosaics. The mask presents a very powerful image, with the angular features stripped down to the minimum.

◄ A modern Akamba mask from Kenya, East Africa made from carved wood, stained and polished.

Insects

On these two pages there are four examples of insects drawn in a combination of materials that suit the colours and textures of the insect.

▲ Stag beetle

The stag beetle has been drawn with a graphite stick blended with a **tortion**, with a touch of crayon for the blue sheen of the shell. White highlights have been left to add to the effect of the hardness and glint of the shell.

▲ Blow fly

The blow fly has been drawn with the same technique as the stag beetle, with the addition of an HB pencil for the wings and shadows.

Pastel & Tortillon   J.L.O. 96

◀ Four-spot ladybird

This ladybird drawing has been drawn with chalk pastels on to coloured sugar paper. Paper-towelling and a tortion have been used to blend the colours, which achieves the smoothness of the shell. Shadows under the insect lift it off the page.

Cockroach ▶

The cockroach has been drawn with coloured pencils on to black paper, which give the colours strength and radiance. Shadows have been added to give a 3D effect. Touches of white gouache have been used for the highlights.

Key word

tortion wound, soft paper

J.L.O. 96

Insects

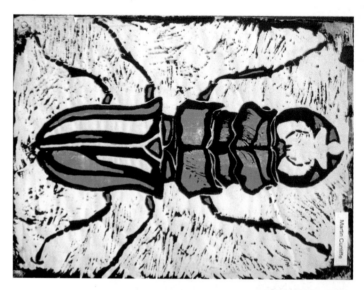

Stag beetle ▶

A two-colour lino-print, using the same block. First the green was printed, then the block was recut for the black overprint.

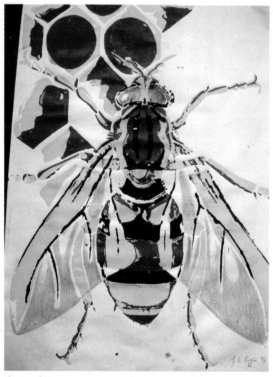

▲ Honey bee

A three-colour silkscreen, using paper masks, with pencil shading for the wings.

▲ Orb spider

A relief-print, using a glue gun for the web, and printed in white on black.

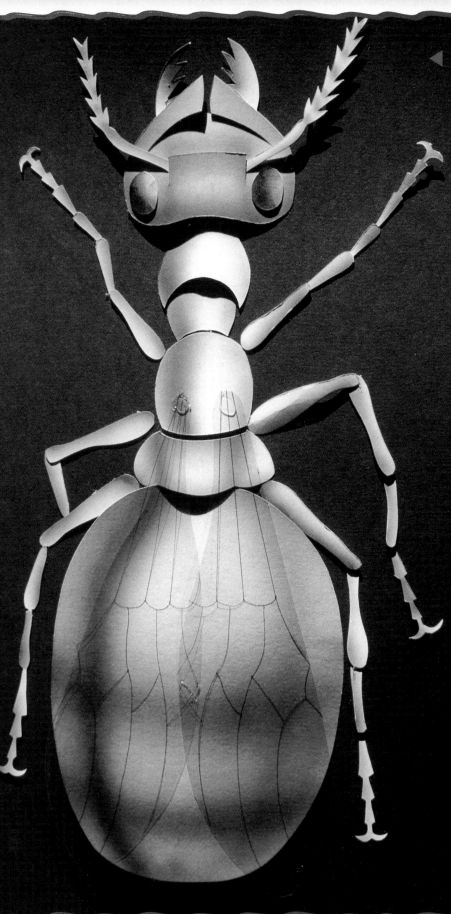

◀ Flying ant

This flying ant was assembled by cutting the various sections out of two-sheet white card, then airbrushing each section with the modulated colour (alternatively, a spray-diffuser could be used). Each section was then glue-gunned to a black base, folding and overlapping each section to create the illusion of form and depth. Acetate was used for the wings and the veins were drawn on with a permanent marker.

Tone and landscape

This page shows a wonderfully atmospheric landscape painting by T'ang Yin. We get a sense of being overpowered by the sheer scale of the peaks on all sides. The figures are tiny in comparison. The swirling mist adds to the sense of atmosphere, as the lofty peaks gradually recede into the distance.

The various elements of the piece have been highly stylized, almost as though the painter followed certain conventions for trees, rocks and people. It is very unlikely that this was painted from life, but from memory, where the artist tried to recapture the effect that the experience had upon him. He has composed the painting to maximize the poetry of the moment.

'Pine trees hanging in the water by a mountain path' by T'ang Yin, pen and wash drawing, c. 1500

The introduction of colour can change the feeling and 'mood' of the composition. Here, blue has been added and has been shaded with black and tinted with white to add to the sense of distance. The introduction of red would have created a totally different feel, such as the warmth of the setting sun.

Tone and landscape

These two field-sketches were made with a water-soluble pencil, with a wash added to introduce soft tones and greys. The top sketch is mainly a rural scene while the bottom one has a more urban content. These sketches were then used as a basis for further development, along with the introduction of Eastern elements.

This page shows a finished composition, based on field-sketches done in the area of Ankerdine Hill, Worcestershire, but now developed with a strong Eastern feel. Distance is suggested by the hills receding in the mist. The pine tree and foreground rocks follow the linear style of the Chinese masters.

ANKERDINE

Glossary

Aquarelle pencils water-soluble pencil crayons

Blending the merging and overlapping of different colours

Brush-drawing painting in a linear style with the tip of the brush

Burnishing adding white or colourless crayon over a coloured area to create a smooth layer, before adding further layers of colour

Ceramic plaque a shallow-relief ceramic sculpture of different levels

Collage an image made up of cut paper pieces pasted on for a tonal or colour effect

Complementary colours colours that are opposite each other on the colour wheel: red and green, purple and yellow, blue and orange

Conté a hard, brittle stick of chalk, ideal for tonal drawings

Continuous line a smooth unbroken line

Cross-hatching lines set at an angle to build up a denser tone or texture

Cross-section an object cut through to show its internal structure

Distressing ageing a support by sponging and stippling, etc.

Figurative design a design consisting of recognizable forms

Frottage an image made by combining rubbings from various textures

Geometric design a design composed of abstract shapes

Gouache thick, opaque watercolour, which dries flat

Graduation a gradual change from one tone to the next

Graphical the combination of type, illustration and layout in a design

Graphite stick a compact strip of graphite with no wood, ideal for dark, tonal shading

Heraldic design a design incorporating details associated with a coat of arms/medieval motifs

Image distortion the way an image is broken up when viewed through glass or water

Incised cut away, scratched or inscribed, with a sharp point or by pressing

In-the-round a 3D sculpture that can be viewed from several angles, not just in relief

Limited palette a restricted range of colours which are intermixed

Lino-print a print taken off the raised, inked-up surface of a piece of linoleum

Mixed media a combination of different materials, e.g. crayon with watercolour

Modelling adding more clay to a shape to build up form, or creating an illusion of 3D by adding tone

Opaque more pigment is used, so that you can't see through the colour

Pattern-repeat where a design has been repeated over an area, often linking together in a continuous pattern

Primary colours the key non-mixed colours: red, yellow and blue

Secondary colours colours mixed by combining two primary colours: orange, purple and green

Shades colours mixed by adding white

Silhouette a shape or figure blacked-out against strong light

Stippling a drawing made up of points or dots

Surrealist movement a group of artists whose work featured real objects placed out of their usual role or in unusual combinations

Template or **mask** a shape cut out of paper, used to duplicate a design or shape as either a negative or a positive image

Tertiary colours colours mixed by combining adjacent secondary and primary colours

Textural describing various surface effects, such as grass, rock and water

Tints colours mixed by adding white

Tone the variation of shading from dark to light

Tortion/tortillon wound, soft paper used as a blending tool

Transparent see-through (e.g. washes that are thinly applied)

Viewfinder a piece of card with a hole cut in it for selecting an area of an image for closer scrutiny

Wash a very watery mix applied with a large brush